FREE BEER TOMORROW

HEIDI HEATH GARWOOD

Recently, my husband and I were in a mountain burger joint with a bar right in the middle of the room. I looked over to see a sign that read,

"Free Beer Tomorrow"

Hmmm.

I kept reading the menu. We ordered our dinner, then I looked back to the sign. My mind could not wrap around it.

Wait...WHAT?

All of a sudden I started laughing uncontrollably. Not only did I get it, *but it was there just for me*.

It was pure recovery.

The promise that if I don't drink that beer today, there will be free beer tomorrow—then when I get to tomorrow, I look at the sign again and know that if I don't drink today, there will be free beer tomorrow.

This makes me giggle just thinking about it.

The sign might as well say,

"One Day At A Time."

DATE: 1-1-11

What a cool date. I love numbers.

My husband gives me a little slip of paper each day with a number written on it, representing how many days I have been sober. He has done this for me since day one. I had 2364 days of sobriety on January 1, 2011.

Not everybody has that kind of support, but I am here to tell you that all recovery people are your number that you carry in your pocket each day you are sober. That is where you will find support.

I am still counting my days of sobriety because that is all I have. Even though I've had over two thousand days of sobriety, I treat every day as if I am on day one—because I'm living my life one day at a time.

Today, I am not in the past nor am I in the future. My sobriety is right now.

I rejoice in today. The very disease wishing to claim my life now provides inspiration to others—to heal and offer hope to those needing a soft place to fall.

"This is the day the LORD has made;
let us rejoice and be glad in it."

Psalm 118:24

W.A.I.T. WHY AM I TALKING

What a great acronym.

I think God gave us dogs to live with us to remind us that we don't always have to communicate with words.

I think my dog reads my mind. I will think *in my mind*, "maybe I should take Diamond for a walk…" I look over and she is getting out of her bed to come to me and see when we are leaving. Wow! Can I act with that kind of obedience to *my* Master when He thinks of me?

Most of the time I am talking myself out of letting God move my mind and heart—thinking up excuses why I can't do it because of this or that.

I would like to be more dog-like, not talking so much, but just seeing, hearing and noticing what God has placed before me. Listening if there is a need, helping when the cry comes out, acting when I am called to go in—even if it's hard.

God, help me to wait. Help me to be more sensitive to hearing You. Help me to be more obedient to your calling.

Amen

FEAR

False **E**vidence **A**ppearing **R**eal

If I look around in the world, I can find all the evidence I need to prove that I should stay in fear. It takes a measure of trust and faith to not buy into the false evidence.

I can't be in fear and faith at the same time.

Fear tells us that we are small, powerless, and separate.

Faith affirms that we are great, creative, and connected.

Which voice do you choose to be your guide?

I am bigger than fear. I *choose* faith as I step forward and live in the light.

Oh God, You paint the morning sky with miracles in mind. My tearful eyes joyfully receive the awesome stroke of your brush.

Thank you for another day of sobriety so that I can see Your wonders before me every day.

LOOKING INTO THE FACE OF GOD

When I have my camera in my hands and I'm shooting the exquisite teal morning waves crashing, I cannot get enough. It is like eating M&M's and drinking ice-cold water. I want the feeling to last forever—I want that goodness and buzz to last. Like the high I sought from alcohol, which I continued to chase and never fully felt again after the first years of drinking but continued to seek in the bottle.

The feeling that I could conquer the world was momentary and temporary, ever-decreasing with every drink I took. The more I sought it in alcohol, the further away it went.

Not until I asked God to help me, did He take away the obsession to drink. He lifted it. God gave me a second chance at life and I was reborn. The old me died, and now the new me can get to the high I sought and beyond.

When I look at the richness of color in the teal wave as a new day dawns, all I can do is rejoice as I stare into the face of God.

Sober. Whole. Reconnected to God and to the person God meant for me to be.

The hole in my soul is filled.

REMINISCING WITH STRANGERS

My brother, Roger, leaned over to me in a meeting and pointed to a saying in his journal that read,

"This is the only place that you can go and reminisce with total strangers."

It took me a while to actually get how powerful that statement was. When alcoholics share their story, other alcoholics can say, "yes, I remember doing that, thinking that, or being that way."

There is no other venue in life that puts us immediately on the same page as our fellow brothers sitting next to us in a meeting. This program is the great equalizer. It has us all holding hands—a doctor standing with an ex-con—while saying the Lord's prayer and smiling together in complete joy and identification with each other—just as God planned.

We need each other.

We are not strangers anymore when the truth is shared.

GOD'S VOICE IS LOUDER THAN MINE

As I was singing along with a praise and worship song the other day, one of the lines stopped me. It went like this:

"God, I need Your voice to be louder than Mine."

Wow.

The truth bell went off in my head while singing that line. So often my committee of voices in my own head crowd out the voice of God.

I need to seek through prayer and meditation to improve my conscious contact with God. That means for me that I need to talk less, listen more.

God speaks to me through other people. He speaks in nature through a beautiful sunset, dolphins playfully skimming over the water, pelicans diving into the ocean for dinner, and looking up the trunk of a majestic old redwood.

He speaks through somebody reaching out for help.

I need to listen to hear God's voice—not be chattering away. When I hear God's voice, it is easier for me to walk in that direction.

IMPATIENCE

Impatience is the fruit of pride and ego.

Think about it.

Impatience focuses on self above all else. When I am impatient with someone else, I am placing my own importance above theirs.

The word impatience derives from the Latin meaning, "not able to bear or suffer."

Yes. I will do anything to not suffer, including push other's needs out of the way before meeting my own. When I think of it that way, I hold the mirror up to see just how selfish I can really be.

To turn this around, I just need to step out and help somebody else. I get out of my own head and decide to put their needs first. In doing that I find my patience level increases.

Imagine that.

By not thinking about myself, I am not suffering anymore. This is the function of service to others.

God is patient with us. He wants to help us not suffer.

SURRENDER

Unparalleled distress can set the stage for unparalleled deliverance.

The toughest things in life that we have to face can be where God does his richest work. If we trust him and turn it over to him just when we think we can't bear it any more, we will be delivered to the other side of it.

The world is filled with paradox. I felt like surrender was "giving up" when, in fact, it was the first step in gaining power back.

The dictionary definition of Paradox is, "Apparently self-contradictory statement whose underlying meaning is revealed only by careful scrutiny. In poetry, *paradox* functions as a device encompassing the tensions of error and truth simultaneously, When a paradox is compressed into two words, as in *living death*, it is called an oxymoron."

I had become an oxymoron. I was alive, but spiritually dead—unable to respond. This is how alcohol was for me. I felt like it made it easier for me to be me. But the truth was that it took me farther away from the real me and from God.

God gave us the power to choose to listen to him or not. Surrendering to His will is not giving up power, but gaining power so that his light will shine in us and through us and light the path for others as well.

The paradox is that we become *more* powerful when we surrender. The power is there at our disposal at all times. All we have to do is surrender to gain power.

JUDGMENT

The Bible tells us not to judge—not because we should not judge, but because we cannot judge—we don't know all the facts. There is only ONE who has that knowledge.

God.

When I judge somebody, I focus on a single moment from one particular angle. At a different moment, I may see a totally different person.

We are also taught to not quit before the miracle. This includes while watching others grow too. I don't want to quit forgiving and cutting them slack before I get to witness the miracle happen in their lives!

Things exist. Situations happen. It is my perception that is askew. Adding my judgment separates me. As I see my part in anything, it becomes clearer what I need to do or how I need to change my thinking. Seeing it as *it is* unites me with life.

When I behold life through the eyes of love, I will find the beauty of God everywhere. I choose to see the world and life through God's vision today.

I focus on loving and let all else go.

JOURNEY INTO THE LIGHT

I don't know if God talks to you, but He does to me—not in words, but fragments of thoughts that come like flashes of light that surprise me. Sometimes they are clear as a bell. Sometimes muddy and ominous. They all come from outside my head, I know, because I can't make up these things.

At times, I get a thought that is totally off subject that surprises me. I immediately say, "Thank you, God. Now what should I do with *that* information?"

If I let go and trust that He will show me as I go about my day, God usually does. I can stay silent and not move and be stuck, or I can act on the thoughts and walk into the Light to serve others and to serve my God.

I walk obediently, God, into service for you today and every day.

> *"For His invisible attributes, that is, His eternal power*
> *and divine nature, have been clearly seen since the creation*
> *of the world, being understood through what He has made*
> *so that men are without excuse."*

Romans 1:20

SAFETY NET

The drink: safety had arrived when the buzz kicked in. NOW I could be myself and not flinch.

Being sober, I have no back-up me. The only me I have is the sober me and I don't always like her. She is not always on. It is hard to always be raw and just there.

No safety net.

Day by day it gets easier.

When I look out there in nature, I see there is no safety net out there either. All animals and plant life are at the effect of their surroundings. They have to trust that nature will not fail them. I see that God made nature for us to observe this phenomenon.

I have to trust that by being me and showing up, throwing my so-called safety net—the drink—aside and trusting God, that it will all be ok.

I will be ok.

I can, not only survive, but thrive. And, hopefully, help others to do the same.

HUMILITY

At the end of my drinking I suffered humiliation. I had embarrassment for things I had done and who I had become. I was hopeless.

I found out that humility is not the same as humiliation.

Humility: Low estimate of one's importance.

Humiliation: Feeling shame or injury to one's dignity or self-respect.

Big difference.

I can have humility and not suffer humiliation.

Being humiliated, I am stuck in victim mode, jealousy, resentment, and fear. You don't even exist for me in that state. It's all about me.

My ego becomes the right size by being humble. I can look at others with respect and rejoice in their victories because mine are not threatened. I set aside my own ego and self-thought to make other's needs important to me.

Today, humility is something I long for and consciously practice.

It serves me well when I am serving.

SPIRIT VS EGO

While passion fueled by Spirit can save our life, passion directed by ego can ruin it.

I have heard it said that "EGO is **E**dging **G**od **O**ut"

So true.

God and I cannot both be in control, or there wouldn't be a relationship. My ego must be deflated and pushed aside to commune with my God.

He is in control.

Have you ever clung to something so passionately and simply could not let go? Perhaps the struggle feels like life and death.

That is how the grip of alcohol felt on me.

I was strong-arming God to say, "I can beat this" (EGO)—when in fact, at the end, I could not stop without His help.

All quality things come to me at the right time by the hand of a gracious God.

CHOOSE FAITH

When I was at the height of my drinking, it was not a choice for me. There was no deciding about it. When things went bad, I couldn't cope, anxiety ruled my emotions, the alcohol was in.

It WAS my solution.

People who don't understand alcoholism say, "Why can't you just stop— decide not to drink?"

What?

There are things we just don't understand. That is where faith comes into play. We have to trust that God has the big picture all managed and we don't know every detail. Besides, if we did, we couldn't control it anyway.

If I could have stopped drinking on my own, I would have. It was only by turning to God and asking Him to remove my obsession, that He did.

> *"Trust in the Lord with all your heart*
> *and lean not on your own understanding;*
> *in all your ways submit to him,*
> *and he will make your paths straight."*

Proverbs 3:5

www.heathdesign.com

Special thanks to my mom, Frieda, who always believed in me, even when I didn't.